# WILLIAM FIELD'S PHOTOGRAPHS OF PUTNEY

Compiled by Dorian Gerhold and Michael Bull
for the Wandsworth Historical Society

**Cover photo:** William Field's shop at 9 Putney High Street in about 1912.

**Inside back and front covers:** Ordnance Survey maps of Putney in 1865, just 13 years before Field began taking photographs of Putney.

**Title page:** Vanderbilt's coach passing into Putney High Street from Putney Bridge, 1909. Alfred Gwynne Vanderbilt was an American with enormous wealth and a love of horses and coaching, who first came to England in 1907. In 1909 he was running two coaches regularly between London and Brighton, driving one of them himself. This picture can be seen in the window of Field's shop on the cover of this book.

**Acknowledgements:** We would like to thank Wandsworth Museum for permission to print many of the photographs in this book from the Museum's collection, and Peter Blackwell for permission to publish Figs. 1 and 6 and for information about Field and his family.

ISBN: 0 905121 06 6
ISSN: 0307 3181

Printed by Roebuck Print Shop, Mitcham

# WILLIAM FIELD, PHOTOGRAPHER, 1854-1932

William Field began photographing Putney in 1878, and his work is the main record of Putney's appearance before it was transformed by suburban development. Much of old Putney was destroyed in the 1880s, within a few years of his arrival, including the last of the great houses of Putney High Street, the old bridge, the old waterfront and many houses and shops. Most of these appear in Field's photographs, without which there would be only a small number of drawings (generally of the church or the bridge or great houses) and a few photographs by others to show us what that earlier Putney was like.

William Field was born on 22 July 1854 at 4 Dennison Place, Mile End. His great-grandfather and grandfather had been butchers (the former being Master of the Butcher's Company in 1822-3) and his father was a tallow salesman (tallow being the fat used to make candles and soap), although by the time of his death he was a commission agent, living in Tottenham. William Field's mother, Julia, died in 1857 and his father, also William Field, in 1864. His grandparents, Samuel and Mary, were still alive (until 1874 and 1873 respectively), and it was probably they who brought up William Field from the age of ten until he was old enough to leave home. He was entitled to a third of his father's estate and, under his grandfather's will, to some freehold property, probably at the age of 21 (i.e. in 1875).

On 18 June 1874 he married Marianne Elizabeth Crispin at St Stephens Church, Hammersmith. He was 19 and she 20. They were already living at the same address - 2 Sterne Street, Shepherds Bush. On the marriage certificate Field is described simply as a clerk. By the following year, when their first child was born, they were living at Lewisham. Three children were born to the couple in Lewisham.

In 1878 Field leased 9 Putney High Street (on the site now covered by the cinema) and established himself there as a photographer, no doubt using his inheritance to do so. Behind the shop, at the end of a yard, was a workshop with a 'photographic room' above, where his photographs were presumably developed and printed. At first he and his family lived above the shop. In 1888 there were kitchen, pantry and parlour on the first floor and two bedrooms on each of the floors above. Two more children were born in Putney, the last in 1887, and one died, leaving four.

Field set up his business at a significant time not only for Putney but for

*1 William and Marianne Field.*

photography. Previously photography had involved cumbersome equipment, disagreeable chemicals and (usually) long exposures to produce 'wet plates', which had to be developed almost immediately. By 1878 'dry plates' were in mass production, and photography had become a much simpler process, involving exposure times only a tenth or twentieth of those of wet plates - as little as a twenty-fifth of a second. Almost all of Field's surviving plates are dry plates.

How much experience Field had of photography is unknown: perhaps he had been a photographer's clerk in Lewisham. Equally, he may have seen the opportunity to establish himself in a new and expanding trade and become his own

**2** An enlargement from a view of 1878, the year Field came to Putney. The window display consists almost exclusively of portraits, which must have provided the bulk of Field's income. The left-hand door presumably led to the accommodation above.
W. Silcock & Co, tailor and draper, provides a typical crowded window display.

**3** Another enlargement, c.1886. The pavement on the right now rises towards the level of the new bridge. In the background meat hangs outside Betts the butcher (later Pook's; see Fig. 26).

**5** Field's premises at 9 Putney High Street, from a sale catalogue of 1888. Field's `photographic room' was over the workshop at the back.

**4** Field's shop and its neighbours in about 1912 (the photograph from which the enlargement on the cover is taken). Field's and Starr's premises probably dated from the seventeenth century. Since 1878, Field has repainted his name-board with bolder lettering, replaced the bay window to provide a larger display space and placed a new window where the left-hand entrance used to be; the level of the pavement has been raised following the building of the new bridge, and tram lines have been laid. The lady in the window with the cat is presumably Marianne Field. On the left, Lambert is demonstrating how large a quantity of fancy and leather goods can be crammed into a single window display, and deliveries of milk are being made from the hand-cart of F.I. Morrison (see Fig. 59). Arthur Case's horse dentistry was presumably not practised in the tiny premises squeezed in between No. 11 and Putney Market.

**6** A sketch made by Field's neighbour, Frederick Starr, following the burst water main at the bottom of Putney High Street on 2 February 1909.

master, choosing Putney as a place without too many competitors. In fact Putney already had at least one professional photographer - Sir Aubrey Paul, baronet, at 1 and 2 Thames Place, Lower Richmond Road - but he is not recorded in the Putney rate books after 1882 and only one of his pictures of Putney is known to survive.

Field only occasionally published his views as postcards; much more often he allowed others to use them on their own postcards. He later stated that he had intended the photographs to be a support for him in his old age, although by that time there was little interest in them. Field shared the Victorian taste for the picturesque, such as Fairfax House or the old bridge, both of which he photographed many times. He showed no interest in eighteenth-century mansions such as Ashbourne House and The Lawn in Putney High Street (both demolished in 1887) or the houses facing Putney Heath. Nor was he interested in the railway, or the process of change: the only views recording demolition and rebuilding are those of the bridge. Some of his photographs were undoubtedly commissions, such as those of shops and their owners. Much of his work would of course have been portraits and group photographs, including those of Boat Race teams.

Field's shop window described him as `photographer and artist'. It is not clear what the `artist' part of the business involved, but he was certainly an accomplished caricaturist. An interest in woodworking is also recorded.

Family tradition is that, while Field had considerable artistic and technical ability, he was a poor businessman. According to his grand-daughter he preferred to undertake quality work and would not compete with those producing cheap photographs; also he failed to obtain payment for much of the work undertaken for crews and students at Boat Races and regattas. He was said to be an unusual man, following whims and somewhat erratic in behaviour.

Field's marriage was not a happy one. In 1901 he left his wife and went to Saskatchewan in Canada, buying land in or near Winnipeg. After a year he sold it and returned to England. By 1906 the Fields were living at 57 Deodar Road instead of above the shop, although they seem to have remained there only until about 1910. At some stage the couple separated, and Marianne lived apart from her husband in Wimbledon until her death in 1937. Field's photographic assistant, known as `Auntie Bobbie' and regarded as a member of the family, came to live with him.

In 1914 Field moved his business to 105-107 Putney High Street (the sixth and seventh shops south from Montserrat Road), a butcher's shop, where his premises were probably on an upper floor. He retired in late 1927 or early 1928. He spent his last few years in lodgings at 18 Burstock Road, and died on 23 October 1932, aged 78. Four children survived him, one of whom, Lennox Field, lived in Putney and was an important figure in Putney rowing until his death in 1956.

Before his death Field sold his Putney photographs to E.P. Olney, a local businessman and amateur photographer. The collection already included a few photographs taken by others, especially several by a chemist called Farmer (including Fig. 12 and probably Fig. 17 in this volume). Olney added greatly to the collection, both through new photographs of his own and copies of older ones. Consequently it is not invariably clear which are Field's. Those in this volume where doubt arises (other than the two by Farmer) are Figs. 57 to 59, 65 and 76.

On Olney's death in 1967 the plates and negatives passed to Douglas Harrod, who put them in good order and made them available to local historians and others. He died in 1994, leaving them to the National Monuments Record. Wandsworth Museum has a full set of prints, and most can also be found in the Local History Collection at Battersea Library.

**A note on dating:** Occasionally a Field photograph carries a date, and a few provide information enabling reasonably precise dating, such as the theatre advertisement in Fig. 27 and the newspaper placard in Fig. 90. Some of those published as postcards are dated, though not reliably. Douglas Harrod's prints are often given dates, but it is not clear on what authority, and the dates can occasionally be shown to be incorrect. In many cases only an approximate date can be given, drawing chiefly on the Putney rate books (in London Metropolitan Archives) and Kelly's directories (for views showing tradesmen's names) and on knowledge of when Putney buildings were built or demolished. Douglas Harrod's dates have been used where there is no reason to doubt them.

**Sources:** Philip Richards, `Field, Marlet or Blake? - a Putney publisher', *Picture Postcard Monthly*, No. 53 (Sept. 1983); family recollections provided by Peter Blackwell; recollections of Peter Gerhold; marriage certificates; will of William Field, 1864, at Somerset House; Putney rate books, 1877-8 (London Metropolitan Archives, P95/MRY1/97 and 98); local directories and electoral lists; sale catalogue of 9-21 Putney High Street, 1888 (in the possession of Dorian Gerhold); Helmut Gernsheim, *The history of photography* (1969).

DJG

**7** The bridge and aqueduct seen from the tower of St Mary's Church in 1881. The bridge was completed in 1729, when it was the only one over the Thames between London Bridge and Kingston. It was demolished in 1886. The present bridge follows the line of the aqueduct (built c.1855), and now carries the pipes. The white building straddling the roadway was the toll-house for the Fulham side. Other buildings on the Fulham side, from left to right, are Pryor's Bank (in front of the church tower; built c.1837; demolished 1897), Thames Bank (demolished 1887), Swan Maltings (built c.1800), and Willow Bank (to the right of the bridge; built in the 1750s; demolished c.1889).

**8** Old Putney Bridge seen from the Putney shore in 1878. In the centre of the bridge is the iron section which replaced three wooden spans in 1871 to provide a wider passage for vessels.

**9** Old Putney Bridge and the Fulham tollhouse on the left and the aqueduct on the right, seen from the Fulham shore.

**10** Old Putney Bridge and the Thames partly frozen in 1881, seen from the Fulham side. The people on the bridge give a good indication of the size of the bridge's wooden piers.

**11** Another scene from the same winter. On the left is Gothic Villa, an early nineteenth-century house demolished in about 1913. In the centre are St Mary's Church and the bridge toll-house, with the bridge's approach road curving round the churchyard. On the centre-right is the White Lion, as rebuilt in 1879 (it was rebuilt again in 1887 with the rest of the block and is currently known as the Slug and Lettuce). On the right is the aqueduct.

**12** The approach to Putney from the bridge, c.1870. The plate is marked 'Farmer's original negative' (Farmer presumably being the chemist who had a shop almost opposite Field's), but it appears to have come into Field's possession and was printed during his lifetime as a photograph taken by Field. It shows the Red Lion Inn, once Putney's main inn but demolished in about 1884 and not rebuilt, and the White Lion Inn, demolished and rebuilt in the late 1870s. The lion above the White Lion appears to have stood on both subsequent buildings.

**13** Paying the toll at Putney in 1880, the year the bridge was freed from toll. The notice on the right states the tolls. Even pedestrians had to pay.

**14** Construction of the new bridge along the line of the former aqueduct, seen from St Mary's Church tower in 1884. The aqueduct pipes have been diverted alongside the old bridge.

**15** The new bridge, seen from the same vantage point. The bridge was widened in 1931-3. On the Fulham side, part of Swan Maltings can still be seen here, but Pryor's Bank has been replaced by the pavilion built in 1899 to provide refreshment facilities, a reading room and staff accommodation for Bishop's Park. The river wall of Bishop's Park was completed and the Park formally opened in 1893.

**16** Removal of the piers of the old bridge in 1886. In the background is the District Railway Pier. The railway had reached Putney Bridge Station in 1880 but the extension across the river towards Wimbledon was not opened until 1889.

**17** The bottom of Putney High Street, c.1868-70. This is probably another photograph by Farmer, since it appears to have been taken from a window above his shop (see Fig. 20). The narrow approach to Old Putney Bridge can be seen, as can a crowded steam-boat on the river. The Rose and Crown pub, occupying what is now the approach to the ICL building, was suppressed as a nuisance in 1887. On the left of the Rose and Crown was the approach to Church Row.

**18** The arch erected at the bottom of Putney High Street to celebrate the freeing of the bridge from toll in June 1880. The church clock shows 9.15; probably it is Sunday morning. 'Velkommen' is Danish: the ceremony of freeing the bridge was performed by the Prince of Wales (later Edward VII) and his wife, Princess Alexandra, who was Danish.

**19** Construction work on the approach to the bridge at the bottom of Putney High Street, c.1885. The man in the centre is outside Field's shop. The split-level pavement seen in Fig. 3 has been laid.

**20** An exceptionally high tide in February 1882, seen from the roof of 3-7 Putney High Street. On the left is a handsome terrace of eighteenth-century shops with attractive shop-fronts, demolished in 1883/4. They included Farmer's shop, from which Fig. 17 was probably taken. The horse-buses are 'knifeboard' buses, so-called from the back-to-back 'knifeboard' seats on top carrying five each side. A further two outside passengers sat either side of the driver and there were 12 insiders.

**21** The end of the Lower Richmond Road seen from the approach to the old bridge in 1881. The Red Lion (on the left), the ancient white buildings with Venetian windows, Bridge Wharf and all the buildings on the riverbank behind it (including the Eight Bells) were swept away in 1882-4 for the approach to the new bridge and the terrace of shops which included the new White Lion. The District Railway notice offers a 32 minute journey between Putney Bridge Station (then the terminus) and Mansion House and omnibuses to Putney meeting all trains.

**22** A detail from Fig 21. Forgotten but essential figures of Victorian London - the street sweepers. Enthusiastic bill-posting in the background.

**23** St Mary's Church and the bottom of Putney High Street seen from the landing place before the construction of the new bridge, c.1882. The approach to the old bridge was between the two walls in front of the church. The waggon on the right is loaded with the old railings which can be seen there in Figs. 21 and 22.

**24** A detail from Fig. 23. In the background on the left is Church Row, a long-established alley of houses on what is now the approach to the ICL building. The man in the centre of the group of three is standing in the approach road to the bridge. The lamp-post on the right is the one on which two men are leaning in Fig 20. The stuccoed terrace of three shops on the right survived until the early 1970s.

**25** An enlargement showing King & Walker's drapery store at 5-7 Putney High Street. King & Walker appear in the rate books from 1880 to 1883.

**26** Pook's butcher's shop at 15 Putney High Street, c.1893. Kelly's directory records William Harriott, whose name is on the delivery tricycle and gig, in 1892 and Mrs E.E. Pook in 1893 and 1894. Pook evidently lived over the shop, as Field did. Pook's premises stretched back to Brewhouse Lane and included slaughter-houses. His house and shop dated from the sixteenth or seventeenth centuries.

**27** Building work at 15 Putney High Street, July 1902, refacing what had been Pook's shop (which had lost its large chimney). The building was demolished only a year or so later in order to build the short-lived Putney Market. The posters for Fulham Theatre reveal the date, by narrowing the possible years to those in which 14 and 21 July were Mondays.

**28** A detail from Fig. 27.

**29** Looking south along the lower end of Putney High Street from just outside the churchyard gate in 1881.

**30** The lower end of Putney High Street from outside No.11, c.1883. The building set back from the street on the right exists today, with three shops built over its garden. On the left, Betts' meat at No. 15 hangs right down to the pavement.

**31** The premises of Stephen Lydiatt, pork butcher and dairyman, in 1882. Lydiatt, who is presumably the man to the right of the doorway, also sold bread and eggs and was agent for the London Parcels Delivery Company. Photography was clearly still sufficiently unusual in 1882 to attract a crowd. The Lydiatts later moved to the Lower Richmond Road, where the family's business continued until the mid-1960s.

**32** A barrel organ in Weimar Street, c.1905, taken from an upstairs window of Field's own premises. It was evidently a sufficiently familiar sight for the children at the other end of the street to be taking no notice of it. In the background are the cottages of Albert Place, built on the site of the parish workhouse, and the newly-built Kenilworth Court.

**33** A detail from Fig. 32. In addition to the music there is clearly something to see, visible from both sides - perhaps some sort of moving image.

**34** Albert Row (roughly on the site of the present Weimar Street), c.1878. These buildings with their large chimneys dated from the seventeenth century. The cottages in the background (Albert Place) are also visible in Fig. 32.

**35** Looking along the Lower Richmond Road (then Windsor Street) from outside St Mary's Church, with the Red Lion on the left, c.1881. Within a few years this part of Putney was completely transformed by the new bridge and associated works.

**36** A detail from Fig. 35.

**37** Looking east along the Lower Richmond Road towards St Mary's Church, 1882. Some demolition has already taken place on the left in preparation for the new bridge (compare Fig. 38). W. Makepeace, tobacconist and hairdresser, appears in the rate books here from 1879 to 1882; later he had premises in Putney High Street. Notices proclaim 'Umbrellas recovered & neatly repaired' and 'Gentlemen waited upon at their own residence'. The dog has remained on its hind legs long enough not to be blurred. The alley to the right, known as Dyos's Platt, originated in the seventeenth century, and later provided access to the parish workhouse.

**38** The view from a little further along the Lower Richmond Road in 1881. On the left is the Eight Bells pub, strongly associated with rowing. On the right is Clyde House, seen in Fig. 40.

**39** The Eight Bells, seen from the partly frozen river in the winter of 1880-1.

**40** Clyde House in the Lower Richmond Road in 1882, the much-altered surviving part of a sixteenth or seventeenth-century mansion. Field is standing in its riverside garden, looking south across the Lower Richmond Road. The direction of the sun indicates that it is early morning.

**41** St Mary's Church, the Eight Bells and the Terrace, seen from Putney Pier, 1881. The towpath, constructed in 1776-7, can be clearly seen.

**42** The Terrace in the Lower Richmond Road in 1880. It was built in about 1800 and demolished in about 1900 to build Kenilworth Court. Another early morning photograph.

**43** An enlargement, showing the Lower Richmond Road from the Terrace to the Dukes Head, c.1881. The gardens on the right probably belonged to the houses in the Terrace.

**44** The riverside seen from the new bridge, probably in 1887. From left to right are the new draw dock with its ramp (which exists today), the Terrace (shored up while new buildings are erected to its left), the Star and Garter, the pier from which Field took several of his photographs, and the boathouses. Behind the boats, building work on the Embankment appears to be beginning.

**45** Barges at Alchin's Wharf, 1880, presumably with Mr Alchin himself or his foreman. The Fulham waterfront can be compared with that shown in Fig. 15. On the far right is the Fulham toll-house.

**46** Barges (Lady Flora and Britannia) near the Eight Bells, seen from the towpath in the early 1880s, before the construction of the Embankment. The main cargo was probably coal.

**47** The barges Lydia and Eliza, off Putney in the 1880s. Lydia is carrying a whole family.

**48** Robinson's Raft, from which boats could be hired, 1878. This photograph, taken from the towpath, provides a good view of the pier and of the Fulham shore before the creation of Bishop's Park. The Star and Garter is just beyond the trees on the left. A steam-boat is moored at the pier.

**49** The Star and Garter, seen from the pier in 1881. Steps lead down from it to the river. The Star and Garter was then a true riverside pub, and one of the centres of Putney rowing. It was rebuilt in about 1900.

**50** Ayling's boathouse, between Ruvigny Gardens and the Embankment, in 1898, probably photographed from a boat. This view was taken soon after Ayling moved to Putney from Vauxhall. There had already been boat-building on the site for at least the preceding century. Ayling's business continued here until the 1980s. The notice to the right announces the intended construction of flats (now Ruvigny Mansions).

**51** One of Field's most evocative views: the boathouses lining the towpath in 1882, before the construction of the Embankment in 1887-8. On the left is the London Rowing Club's boathouse, built in 1871 and the headquarters of the National Rowing Association (founded in 1882 and later renamed the Amateur Rowing Association).

**52** The same scene in 1906. By that date the London Rowing Club's boathouse had been enlarged to its present size (compare Fig. 51).

**53** Citizens of Putney enjoying the Embankment on an afternoon in 1913, without the presence of a single motor car. Taken from the balcony of a house shown in Fig. 52.

**54** Eighteenth-century cottages in the Lower Richmond Road, on the north side of the road between Spring Passage and Ruvigny Gardens, 1895.

**55** The Cricketers, Lower Richmond Road, c.1896. Painted on the pub itself is another name - The Cyclist's Rest. There is a long history of cricket on Putney Lower Common, dating back at least to 1800. Jesse Gillett, the landlord, appears in Kelly's directory from 1895 to 1897.

**56** West Lodge (on the left) and Elm Lodge, on Putney Lower Common, seen from the south-west, c.1900. The site, entirely surrounded by common land, was enclosed in the 1760s. The author, Douglas Jerrold, lived at West Lodge from 1845 to about 1854, and entertained there the great literary figures of the day, including Charles Dickens. The site is now occupied by Putney Hospital, opened in 1912.

**57** Morrison's Farm, by the Lower Common south-east of All Saints' Church, seen from the south in 1890.

**58** The back of Morrison's Farm, showing its somewhat flimsy construction. The photographer is standing on what is now the tennis courts between All Saints' Church and Erpingham Road.

**59** F.I. Morrison's dairy, facing the Lower Common just north of All Saints' School, with dairyman's cart, seven three-wheeled hand-carts and a milk float - almost certainly Morrison's entire 'fleet'. Organising a photograph like this was a spectacle which brought the neighbours to their windows. The sign in the window promises 'absolutely pure milk'. Morrison kept his own herd of cows in Putney. Neither the dairy nor the houses to its right exist today.

**60** W. Quenby, 'cash butcher', 1902. The shop stood just west of the junction between Walkers Place and Felsham Road. 'Cash butcher' meant that meat could not be obtained on account. Meat is hung under the ivy with a fine disregard for hygiene. Quenby had managed Stiff's shop, which can be seen in Fig. 74.

**61** Putney Bridge Road (then Wandsworth Lane), looking towards Wandsworth not far from Putney High Street, c.1880. In the centre is the Castle, since rebuilt twice. On the left is an example of the poorer type of building in Putney - timber-framed with brick infill. On the right is the back of Cromwell House, shown in Fig. 62. Everything in this scene has since vanished except for one of the gateposts in the distance, which can still be seen built into the wall of the first shop beyond the present Castle.

**62** The rear of Cromwell House, 1881. This house, probably built about 1700, stood on the south side of Putney Bridge Road opposite the Castle. Evidently it was about to be demolished when this view was taken.

**63** The Castle in 1913. The building is the same as in Fig. 61, but the road has been widened and tram-lines have been laid.

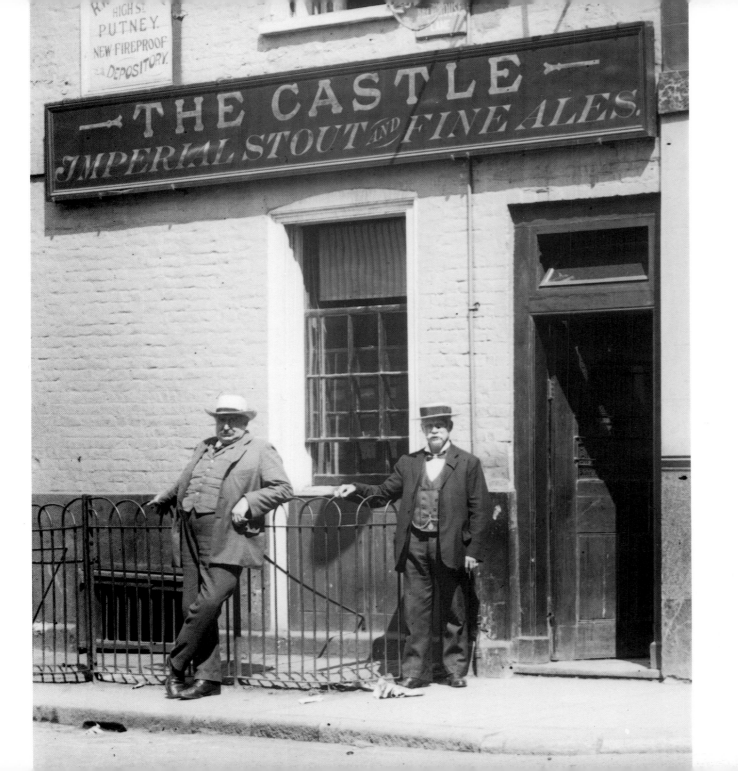

**64** A detail from another view of the Castle taken on the same day as Fig. 63.

**65** Looking west in Putney Bridge Road towards the Castle, with a timber-clad cottage on the right.

**66** Detail from a view in Brewhouse Lane of 1912, showing the family occupying the cottage almost adjacent to the Castle, whose railings can be seen in the background.

**67** A cottage on the east side of Brewhouse Lane, probably built about 1700, in 1912. In the background is Douglas's Wharf.

**68** The Watermen's School (Southfield House), on the south side of Putney Bridge Road about where it is now crossed by the District Railway. The school was established under the will of Thomas Martyn, who died in 1684, to educate twenty sons of watermen. After years of legal wrangling it opened in these magnificent premises in 1718. The schoolhouse was demolished for the District Railway in 1889, but the school carried on elsewhere until 1911 and the charity continues as an educational trust.

**69** The Cedars in 1880 - two terraces of magnificent houses, built in 1853 between what is now Deodar Road and the river and intended to form part of a larger development. There were communal gardens between the terraces and the river. The District Railway was later built through the middle, demolishing three of the houses in the process, and the close proximity of a shrieking steam railway was probably what caused the demolition of the whole of the two terraces in 1890.

**70** The western terrace of the Cedars, seen from in or near Putney Bridge Road in 1881, showing its poor state of repair.

**71** A fallen tree at the Cedars, 1881.

**72** The west side of Putney High Street, looking towards the aqueduct and Fulham Church (in the distance) from between Felsham and Lacy Roads, c.1881. On the extreme left is the entrance to Pepper Alley, created in the seventeenth century, which is probably when the building over the entry was constructed. The Bull and Star is in the centre of the picture, and Felsham Road (then Gardeners Lane) enters the High Street just in front of the furniture warehouse, which probably also dated from the seventeenth century. All the buildings shown here have since been demolished.

**73** A detail from Fig. 72.
W. Turner, general dealer, appears
to be selling second-hand clothes.

**74** The Bull and Star, almost on the corner of Felsham Road and Putney High Street, as decorated for Queen Victoria's Diamond Jubilee in 1897. The building dated from 1692, and was rebuilt a few years after this photograph was taken. Note the two splendid lamps. On the left of the picture, Stiff's sign-board has completely concealed the upper storey of a tiny shop (see Fig. 73).

**75** Looking north along Putney High Street towards St Mary's Church (in the distance), c.1883. Lacy Road (then Coopers Arms Lane) can be seen joining the High Street just before the first lamp-post on the left. The angle of sunlight indicates that this photograph was taken in the early afternoon, in which case it may give a realistic indication of the level of traffic in the High Street; Field has set up his tripod in the middle of the road. The second shop from the right-hand side still exists today.

**76** This photograph was probably not by Field, and may date from a few years before his arrival in Putney. In the centre is the Parsonage - not in fact ever occupied by a parson, but forming part of the same holding as the tithe barn, which stood at the back of the yard to its left. The barn and these two houses were replaced by a terrace of shops in the late 1870s. The shop on the extreme left of the picture still exists.

**77** Looking north along Putney High Street from near the present junction with Montserrat Road, 1880. On the right is the Victorian terrace which replaced the Parsonage, and beyond it the small terrace of earlier shops from which several have survived to the present. On the left are some fine eighteenth-century houses and the two wings of Astley House (see Fig. 78).

**78** The doorways of Astley House, on the west side of Putney High Street a little south of Lacy Road, probably dating from the late seventeenth century.

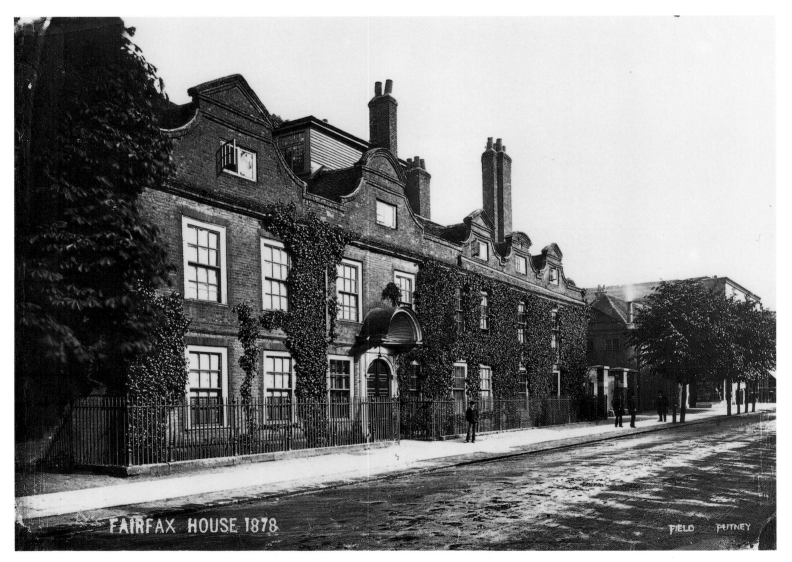

FAIRFAX HOUSE 1878

FIELD PUTNEY

**79** Fairfax House in 1878. This was a red-brick house probably dating in part from the 1630s and in part from about 1700. It was one of the last mansions to survive in the High Street, and a campaign to save it was waged unsucessfully prior to its demolition in 1887. Montserrat Road now enters the High Street about where its fine shell-porch can be seen in this view. The porch survives as part of a house in West Hampstead. Beyond the house can be seen its stables and (visible just above the trees) Putney's Assembly Rooms (now W. H. Smith).

**80** Fairfax House, Putney High Street, 1880-1. Beyond the house is the terrace which replaced the Parsonage.

**81** The side and rear of Fairfax House, seen from its yard in 1884.

FAIRFAX HOUSE 1878

**82** The back of Fairfax House in 1878, showing the join between the original house and the extension to its left. It had a fine garden extending back as far as Burstock Road.

**83** The staircase of Fairfax House, a rare example of an interior view by Field.

**84** The Spotted Horse, as decorated for Queen Victoria's Diamond Jubilee in 1897, with a carefully-posed spotted horse outside. The woodwork which currently decorates the pub dates from much later. The arch on the right led to a small court of four tenements known as Wiggins Court.

**85** Looking north along Putney High Street from just south of Norroy and Disraeli Roads, 1904. Salisbury Pavement (on the left), together with Norroy and Chelverton Roads, replaced Putney High Street's last two mansions in 1887. If the clock has been properly maintained, it is 8.35 in the morning, which is consistent with the direction of the sunlight.

**86** The crossroads of Putney High Street, Putney Hill and the Upper Richmond Road, seen from almost outside Putney Station in 1880. The Fox and Hounds, rebuilt in 1870, claims here to have been established in 1541, though the earliest it can be traced is 1617. The sign saying 'Oxford House' indicates its use by the Oxford team at the time of the Boat Race. The Railway Hotel on the right was established in 1857 and rebuilt later in the century. It had a music hall at the back seating a hundred, where there were performances two or three times a week. Next to the Fox and Hounds are dining rooms (later a pub) called the Duke of Edinburgh. The street frontage on the corner with Putney Hill has since been set back, and all the buildings in this view have been demolished except the Fox and Hounds.

**87** A detail from Fig. 86.

**88** The Duke of Edinburgh, also shown in Fig. 86. Scratched on the plate is the information that it was taken at 5.30 a.m. on 2 July 1895. It was presumably commissioned by James Braid in advance of rebuilding, which took place in 1895. The Duke of Edinburgh closed in the 1970s, though the new building of 1895 survives. By 1895 the Fox and Hounds (on the right) has become even more boastful and inaccurate about its origins, now claiming a date of 1360. Immediately left of the Duke of Edinburgh the tobacconist displays a large 'plug' as the sign of his trade.

**89** The Fox and Hounds, Marshall's stables and numerous advertisements, 1897.

**90** Marshall's Livery & Bait Stables, November 1897. This view can be dated exactly by means of the newspaper hoarding on the left announcing the death of Baron Pollock. 'Job master' meant that Marshall offered horses and carriages for hire for riding or driving - the best option for families which only needed a horse or carriage occasionally. 'Livery stables' meant that Marshall would contract to keep a customer's own horse and possibly carriage for an agreed charge by the week, month or year. 'Bait stables' meant that a customer who wanted to pay a call in the neighbourhood could leave his horse with Marshall for the hour or the day and the horse would be looked after and fed as required.

**91** The Railway Hotel, rebuilt in 1888-9, as decorated for Queen Victoria's Diamond Jubilee in 1897.

**92** Looking west along the Upper Richmond Road from its junction with Putney High Street, 1904. Field appears to be standing in the middle of the crossroads. Drivers are exhorted to 'Keep to the left' and 'drive slowly'.

**93** Looking north along Putney Hill from its junction with St John's Avenue, 1904. The houses on the right dated from the late 1860s. At the time of this photograph the poet Charles Swinburne lived with Theodore Watts Dunton in one of the semi-detached pair third from the right (which still stands).

**94** The Green Man, 1906. The pub dates from the early eighteenth century.

**95** Tibbetts Corner, 1898.

**96** The south facade of Ashburton House, Putney Heath (east of Exeter House), 1895. The boy and girl were presumably the children of John Carlisle, a ship-owner, who occupied the house from 1894 to 1903. The house dated from about 1854 and was demolished in about 1950 to make way for the Ashburton Estate.

**97** St Margaret's Church, c.1890. The church began life in the 1870s as a Baptist chapel, but by the time of this picture was being used by the Presbyterians. Later the Church of England acquired it and named it St Margaret's. The Anglicans built a new chancel, levelled the floor (originally sloping like a theatre) and removed the steps at the entrance. This photograph brings out well the isolated position of the church; beyond it, on the opposite side of Putney Park Lane, can be seen open land belonging to Putney Park - not covered by the Dover House Estate until the 1920s.

**98** The day the foundation stone of Holy Trinity Church, Roehampton, was laid, 10 April 1897. This is one of a series of photographs; by the time of this one the stone has been laid and all the activity is taking place to the left of the picture. In the background is the boys' school (now the infants' school).

**99** Holy Trinity Church, Roehampton, and the girls' school, seen from the east, 1900. The girls' school had been rebuilt in 1877 and 1890, and the church dated from 1896-8. The bicycle leaning against the fence on the left was probably Field's.

**100** The Kings Head, 1904. The earliest parts of the Kings Head probably date from the late seventeenth century. The Kings Head has since lost the tree and much of its forecourt, but the building remains as shown here.

**101** Roehampton Lane, the fountain and the Montague Arms, 1900. The fountain was designed by Sir Frederick Lance for Mrs Lyne Stephens of Grove House, and was built in 1882. The sculpture in the centre was modelled on an Italian tomb and cast in Paris. The trees on the left are in the grounds of Manresa House, then occupied by the Jesuits.

**102** A detail from Fig. 101. The Montague Arms is a mid-eighteenth-century building, but only became a drinking establishment in the 1860s. The shop on the right has since been demolished, but the Montague Arms survives.

**103** A detail from a view of the fountain.

**104** Medfield Street, the Earl Spencer and Roehampton Lane, 1904. The Earl Spencer was first licensed in 1868.

**105** Looking north along Roehampton Lane from its junction with Clarence Lane, 1904. On the left is the lodge and gateway to Grove House, then still a private house, and in the distance are buildings belonging to the Convent of the Sacred Heart. The wall on the right belonged to Roehampton House (now part of Queen Mary's University Hospital).